W9-BOM-866

Goals and Goal Setting

Achieving Measured Objectives

Third Edition

Larrie Rouillard

A Crisp Fifty-Minute™ Series Book

This Fifty-Minute™ book is designed to be "read with a pencil." It is an excellent workbook for self-study as well as classroom learning. All material is copyright-protected and cannot be duplicated without permission from the publisher. *Therefore, be sure to order a copy for every training participant through our Web site, www.axzopress.com.*

Goals and Goal Setting

Achieving Measured Objectives

Third Edition

Larrie Rouillard

CREDITS:
VP, Product Development: **Matt Gambino**
Prodution Editor: **Genevieve McDermott**
Production Artists: **Nicole Phillips, Rich Lehl, and Betty Hopkins**

Trademarks
Crisp Fifty-Minute Series is a trademark of Axzo Press.

Some of the product names and company names used in this book have been used for identification purposes only and may be trademarks or registered trademarks of their respective manufacturers and sellers.

Disclaimer
We reserve the right to revise this publication and make changes from time to time in its content without notice.

ISBN 10: 1-56052-677-7
ISBN 13: 978--56052-677-3
Library of Congress Catalog Card Number 2002106515
Printed in the United States of America
6 7 09 08

Learning Objectives For:

GOALS AND GOAL SETTING

The objectives for *Goals and Goal Setting, Third Edition* are listed below. They have been developed to guide the user to the core issues covered in this book.

THE OBJECTIVES OF THIS BOOK ARE TO HELP THE USER:

1) Understand the meaning of the terms *mission, goal,* and *objective*

2) Explore management/individual negotiations in setting goals

3) Discover how to reach goals

4) Learn ways to translate theory into practice

ASSESSING PROGRESS

A Crisp Series **assessment** is available for this book. The 25-item, multiple-choice and true/false questionnaire allows the reader to evaluate his or her comprehension of the subject matter.

To download the assessment and answer key, go to www.axzopress.com and search on the book title.

Assessments should not be used in any employee selection process.

About the Author

Larrie Rouillard is founder and president of Learning and Resources Co., of Oklahoma City, Oklahoma, a consulting company that specializes in serving the needs of small businesses. Larrie conducts business skills assessments, identifies areas for operational improvement, works with individuals who need specific skill development, and conducts classes on goal setting, negotiating, and strategic planning. Learning and Resources Co. also conducts export plan development seminars. Larrie is a certified Export Plan Developer.

Larrie can be contacted at:

Learning and Resources Co.
8700 South Council Road
Oklahoma City, OK 73169
(405) 745-5002
Fax (405) 745-3740

Dedication

To Tina, my purpose and my strength; to Richard and Carolyn, my guides and role models; and to Travis and Brian—may they find an honorable life mission and make their mark through goal achievement.

Preface

The question I'm most often asked by readers of *Goals and Goal Setting* is, What caused you to write this book, and why goals as the subject?

The truth is, it didn't start out as my idea. A former boss of mine realized most of our staff didn't know how to formally and effectively set and achieve business goals, so he assigned me the task of creating a fundamental, easy-to-use, and repeatable goal-setting structure for our organization. This book evolved from his idea and my original 20-plus-page internal goal-setting training manual.

Looking back on that assignment made me realize that many of the goals we set out to achieve often do not start as our own ideas. Rather, some of our achievements begin as tasks dictated by someone else—a family member, boss, customer, or client. But while a certain goal may not start out as our idea, how we adopt and adapt it as our own are often critical to success.

The first edition of this book partially covered this topic in the "Top-Down/Bottom-Up" goal-setting process discussion. In the second edition, I took the position that the bottom-up method was better for producing maximum commitment to goal achievement. This third edition continues to evolve the discussion by focusing on how to make a goal your own even when it is imposed, assigned, or directed by someone else. In the end, regardless of whether the goal was derived top-down or bottom-up, by you or by someone else, you ultimately have to make the goal *yours* if you want to achieve it.

I've also added a segment on the power of visualization and its effects on motivation and execution, as well as updated examples that are more in line with the most current thinking on the goal-setting and achievement process. Today there are many more goal-setting resources to draw upon than when I created the original training program. Therefore, I've included an additional reading section that presents other perspectives on the goals and goal-setting process.

I hope you find the new additions helpful to your personal goal-setting process and that my book helps you achieve goals that bring you security, prosperity, and happiness!

Larrie A. Rouillard

Larrie Rouillard

How to Use This Book

This *Fifty-Minute™ Series Book* is a unique, user-friendly product. As you read through the material, you will quickly experience the interactive nature of the book. There are numerous exercises, real-world case studies, and examples that invite your opinion, as well as checklists, tips, and concise summaries that reinforce your understanding of the concepts presented.

A Crisp Learning *Fifty-Minute Book* can be used in a variety of ways. Individual self-study is one of the most common. However, many organizations use *Fifty-Minute Books* for pre-study before a classroom training session. Other organizations use the books as a part of a systemwide learning program—supported by video and other media based on the content in the books. Still others work with Crisp Learning to customize the material to meet their specific needs and reflect their culture. Regardless of how it is used, we hope you will join the more than 20 million satisfied learners worldwide who have completed a *Fifty-Minute Book*.

Contents

Introduction

A sense of accomplishment is one of the more satisfying pleasures a person can experience. Beating the competition to market with a new product, landing that big account after months of hard work, or finally getting rid of a nasty habit are examples of things that people delight in achieving.

To be successful, you have to work hard, be a problem solver, and use your creativity and imagination to develop new products and ideas. Each achievement along the way does not happen by accident–it is an outcome of a larger success pattern. Careful planning, thoughtful strategy, and faithful and consistent execution are all factors of success. Also, successful individuals are focused and determined. For them, success is a self-fulfilling prophecy.

Before actions are taken, a goal must exist. A goal could be personal or professional, or it could be a team's common purpose. It is the point that you or the team must reach. Setting a goal that really motivates is not as easy as it sounds. However, you should not think of goal setting as too difficult to be worth your while. A goal's extraordinary power over the direction of your business or personal life is what makes goal setting essential.

This workbook addresses that important process. You will find activities that focus on what a goal is and how to set goals that you can achieve. Step by step, you will practice how to:

➤ Differentiate between goals, missions, and objectives

➤ Follow a technique for establishing goals

➤ Construct objectives

➤ Execute the tactics needed

➤ Achieve your goals

Experience tells us that to learn a process, we have to practice, and that is made easier when we know our purpose. Discovering the purposes for goals and goal setting is the first step in learning these new skills. Let's begin on the next page.

The Purpose of Goal Setting

The first question you might ask about goal setting is, What's in it for me? To answer this question, the discussion of goals and goal setting has been separated into several topics to make it easier for you to understand what a goal is, and how to picture the process needed to set organizational, business, or personal goals.

To begin to think about the purpose of goal setting, think of the questions reporters ask themselves when writing a story:

What?	→	To identify goals
Why?	→	To learn the importance of goal setting in achieving success
Who?	→	To distinguish the people involved in the goal-setting process
Where?	→	To locate opportunities for useful goals
How?	→	To effectively reach goals; to accomplish what you want to achieve

The only question missing is *when*. You are the best person to answer that question.

Remember, these objectives are interrelated. Once you understand these purposes, you will see that setting and achieving goals are essential to success in business as well as in life.

WHAT DO YOU THINK?

Look over the following list and check (✔) yes or no depending on whether you consider the item a goal.

	Yes	No
Increasing sales and profits	❑	❑
Improving productivity in your department	❑	❑
Managing work time more effectively	❑	❑
Seeing the Eiffel Tower in Paris	❑	❑
Capturing the business of an important client	❑	❑
Reducing operating expenses in a critical area in the organization	❑	❑
Being a vice-president in your company	❑	❑
Developing a new product within an allotted budget	❑	❑
Learning to play the piano	❑	❑
Gaining market share for your primary product	❑	❑

In the space below, write what you think are the similarities among the items in the list. Example: *These are all things that people have shown can be done.*

_____

_____

_____

What Do All These Things Have in Common?

If you found all of the items on the list are achievable goals, then you might ask yourself questions like these:

Why can't I . . . ?

Why haven't I . . . ?

Why don't I . . . ?

The answer may be that:

➤ You have no real desire to . . . (manage your time more effectively, be a vice-president, or do what's necessary to capture that new client). If you lack desire to do something, then achieving a goal solely for the sake of achieving it will not motivate you enough, nor will you get the same sense of accomplishment.

➤ You don't know how to establish motivating, stimulating, functional, and executable goals.

If you want to improve department productivity, develop that new product within budget, or see the Eiffel Tower, then you must learn how to set meaningful goals and establish executable objectives that will help you reach those goals. On the following pages you will find information and activities that survey the basics of goal identification, formulation, and execution.

Why Set Goals?

Goals are an essential part of successfully conducting business and living a rewarding life. Well-defined goals allow you to choose, design, and implement important targets (objectives) necessary to achieve overall desired results (missions).

Goals:

➤ Establish **direction** for ongoing activities

➤ Identify **expected** results

➤ Improve **teamwork** through a common sense of purpose

➤ Heighten performance levels by setting **targets** to be achieved

Goals provide the motivation and direction necessary for growth and success in many important areas. In business, for example:

➤ If you or your organization never sets goals for direction, how will you know where you are headed?

➤ If no goals exist for progress, how will your organization know how it is doing?

➤ If there are no goals for achievement, how will the organization know when it succeeds?

Question: *Would you get on an airplane if you didn't know where it was going to land?*

What Is a Goal?

2

Definition of a Goal

> A **goal** is an end toward which you direct **specific effort**.

In this context the end is an exact and tangible result toward which you are willing to expend effort to achieve. What kind of and how much effort is always related to the goal itself, that is, you must be able to identify the cost-and-benefit relationship. Planning and analyzing the steps involved in reaching your goal helps you calculate this relationship.

Elements of a Goal

➤ **An accomplishment to be achieved**

What do I expect the outcome of my (our) actions to be?

In most cases you will want to express this accomplishment with an action verb.

For example: *I want to reduce operating expense in my department from 2% of sales to 1.5%.*

➤ **A measurable outcome**

How will I know when I have reached the outcome?

What are the signs I need to see so I know I have reached the goal?

The situation surrounding the accomplishment has to include things you can use to determine you have reached the goal—simple, identifiable signs of success.

For example: *Operating expense was 2% in June, 1.9% in July, and is now 1.65% in August. The expenses are heading in the right direction.*

➤ **A specific date and time to accomplish the goal**

When do I want to have the goal completed?

Just as important as the other elements are a specific date and time by which you will want to say you have accomplished your goal.

For example: *Reduce business expenses not to exceed 1.5% of total sales for this year.*

➤ **A maximum cost (money, time, and resources)**

What is the maximum cost (money, time, and resources) I will allow myself to achieve this goal?
How much will my efforts have cost me when I say, 'I've done it'?

The cost and resource constraint forces you to place a financial value on the outcome.

For example: *This reduction in operating expense will be achieved with current headcount and without lowering existing service standards.*

These elements help to develop the definition of a goal even further. Below is an expanded definition:

> A **goal** is a **specific and measurable accomplishment** to be achieved within a **specified time** and under **specific cost constraints.**

Goals Must Be Written!

Writing goals down in black and white results in more explicit statements of intent. Daydreaming about your goals does not help you reach them. Writing your goals down strengthens your commitment.

Look at these written goals.

➤ *Increase* productivity in our division 5% by August 15, without adding any personnel

➤ *Gain* five new customers and increase gross sales to $20,000 by July 1 within an expense budget of $1,000

➤ *Expand* market share to 5% by December 31, without increasing advertising expense beyond current levels

➤ *Secure* two clients by June 30 that will produce $30,000 income and require only 30% of my time to service

➤ *Retire* from work and relocate to a warm-climate location

You might think the first and last statements have some fuzzy elements to them. Do they have all the elements they need to be considered goals? What about the other three?

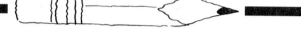

IDENTIFY THE GOAL ELEMENTS

Identify the goal elements in each of the following statements:

1. Gain five new customers and increase gross sales to $20,000 by July 1 with an expense budget of $1,000.

   Action verb:_____

   _____

   Measurable outcome:_____

   _____

   Specific date:_____

   _____

   Cost or resource constraint:_____

   _____

2. Expand market share to 5% by December 31, without increasing advertising expense beyond current levels.

   Action verb:_____

   _____

   Measurable outcome:_____

   _____

   Specific date:_____

   _____

   Cost or resource constraint:_____

   _____

CONTINUED

3. Secure two clients by June 30 who will produce $30,000 of income and require no more than 30% of my time to service.

Action verb:_____

Measurable outcome:_____

_____

Specific date:_____

_____

Cost or resource constraint:_____

_____

Compare your answers with the author's suggested responses in the back of the book.

PRACTICE WRITING A GOAL

With practice, you will learn to easily recognize the elements of a goal. Since you now know what these are, start practicing this skill by writing a simple goal using the elements listed on the previous pages.

_____

_____

_____

_____

_____

_____

_____

_____

_____

_____

_____

_____

_____

_____

_____

_____

_____

_____

_____

Missions

One of the purposes of this workbook is to help you distinguish between missions, goals, and objectives. Knowing the differences between these three related types of statements will help you formulate better goals and achieve better, more profitable results. Here's how these relationships work:

➤ Missions are general intents

➤ Goals are specific and measurable accomplishments to be achieved

➤ Objectives are tactics that you will use to reach and achieve goals

> A mission is a general statement through which a person specifies the overall strategy or intent that governs the goals and objectives.

An organizational mission statement interprets your organization's "reason for being." It enables you to clarify your business purpose both for yourself and others. Here are some examples of different types of mission statements:

Business: Be the recognized world leader in widget sales.

Athletic: Be a Super Bowl contender.

Personal: Travel on the European continent.

In business, a good mission statement should:

➤ Clearly state the nature of your cause

➤ Define your areas of concentration

➤ Identify the markets you serve

➤ Describe your organization's direction

➤ Indicate your general plan for getting there

Do you know your organization's mission? Write it here.

_____

_____

_____

_____

Formulating a mission is an essential part of the goal-setting process. A mission focuses the direction and the efforts for reaching the goals and objectives that follow.

An example of a personal mission is: *Be a role model and make a positive contribution to my community and country.*

Any and all goals and objectives developed must include actions and activities that will complement and contribute to the fulfillment of this mission.

One possible complementary goal could be: *Get a medical degree from a leading institution and a Ph.D. in cancer research by age 35 and work to find a cure for cancer in my lifetime.*

Effective goals complement the overall mission. If you had no mission and no sense of direction, it would be difficult to establish any meaningful goals.

A different mission would require different goals.

For example, another mission might be: *Take an active leadership role in protecting our natural resources and environment.*

What are some possible complementary goals for this mission? Write them here.

_____

_____

_____

_____

A Comment About Missions

The creation of a corporate mission statement requires careful thought and extensive planning. Every aspect of the organization should be touched by the sense of purpose and direction described in the mission statement. Most important, the work of the organization must contribute to the fulfillment of the mission.

A well-prepared mission statement should reflect what the organization—its employees and managers—stands for. It should also describe how customers are treated, as well as how individuals within the organization relate to one another. Ideally, the mission statement guides management style and directs how people are rewarded, trained, and developed.

One fundamental problem plaguing many organizations is the lack of an effective mission statement. As a result, employees have no clear direction or sense of purpose and no desire to create unity, loyalty, and commitment to organizational success. Without a mission statement for direction, any goals created may represent only busywork rather than productive and profitable activity that moves the organization forward.

Objectives

You have examined the elements needed for goal statements and learned how mission statements use these elements. The next step is to learn how the elements work in establishing objectives.

> The **objectives** are **tactics** you use that are **complementary** to the goal, just as goals must be complementary to the mission.

For example, if the mission and goals are:

Mission: *Be a role model and make a positive contribution to the community.*

Goals: *Become a medical research scientist.*

Then complementary objectives might be:

Excel in high school studies.

➤ Enroll in classes which support premed studies

➤ Focus on biology, chemistry, and mathematics

Identify undergraduate and postgraduate institutions.

➤ Determine an area of research interest

➤ Identify institutions that specialize in the chosen area of interest

➤ Research potential institutions to narrow choices

➤ Visit likely candidate schools

Apply to chosen undergraduate schools.

➤ Complete application forms

➤ Solicit letters of recommendation from school, community, and work references

➤ Prepare for interviews

Use undergraduate studies as postgraduate platform.

➤ Choose courses in area of interest

➤ Apply for a summer intern position in a specific research firm

➤ Identify a role model/mentor connected to medical research

These objectives are the steps to be taken to reach the goal. They determine how fast or slow the goal is reached and what methods will be used to achieve the goal.

Goals and Objectives Pyramids

A pyramid is a good visual illustration of the relationship between missions, goals, and objectives. It can also represent the varied approaches used to achieve goals.

The relationship between objectives and goals depends on which approach best satisfies the specific needs for goal achievement and/or your personal preference for reaching the goal. There are three possible relationships between goals and objectives:

1. Several objectives to achieve one goal

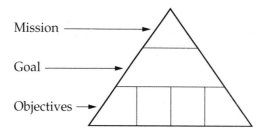

2. One objective to achieve one goal

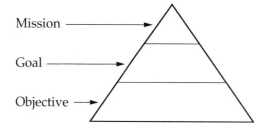

3. Several objectives to achieve several goals

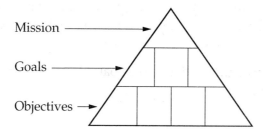

Choosing the approach that most appropriately fits your desired goals will help you reach them.

Summary: What Is a Goal?

> A goal is an end toward which you direct specific effort.

The elements of a goal are:

➤ An accomplishment to be achieved

➤ A measurable outcome

➤ A specific date and time to accomplish the goal

➤ A maximum cost (money, time, and resources)

An expanded definition of a goal would be:

A goal is a specific and measurable accomplishment to be achieved within specified time, resource, and cost constraints.

A written goal provides a strong statement of your intent and the results to be achieved. Goal statements contain these elements:

➤ Action verbs

➤ Measurable outcomes

➤ Specific dates

➤ Cost or resource constraints

A mission statement defines an individual, an organization, or a business. It should describe an overall intent and clarify a reason for being. Goals must be complementary to the fulfillment of the stated mission.

Objectives are tactics used to reach and achieve goals. They must also be complementary to the goals of the mission.

16

Who Sets Goals?

Who Sets Goals Is Important

Who sets goals can be as important to the end result as any other element involved in the process. This is because business goals are achieved through the efforts of individuals who make up teams or groups dedicated to fulfilling the mission. Without personal commitment and effort, goals cannot be achieved.

First and foremost, everyone must be motivated. Motivation is the key to creating the commitment to do whatever is needed to reach the goal and fulfill the mission.

> **Individual + Motivation = Commitment**

Each individual responsible for goal achievement must find the personal motivation to put forth the effort required to achieve the goal. Participation in the goal-setting process is the surest method for motivating individuals into committing to the goal's achievement because people are more committed to reaching the goals they helped create.

Active participation in the goal-setting process includes:

➤ Defining the accomplishment

➤ Determining the specific, measurable outcomes

➤ Creating the timeline of activities and deadlines for completion

➤ Identifying the money, time, and other resources needed for goal achievement

Active participation produces ownership that reflects the internal desire and commitment of individuals.

Management's Role

The goal-setting process should be an individual process, but management must take an active role in guiding, directing, and managing both the goal-setting and the goal-achievement processes. Goal setting should include a negotiation between the people who are responsible for accomplishing the goal (the committed individuals) and those who would like to see the goals achieved (management).

Management is responsible for ensuring the goal-setting negotiation process meets two important requirements:

➤ The goal agreed to is complementary to the corporate or department mission, i.e., achievement of the goal is consistent with, and will move the organization closer to, mission fulfillment

➤ All parties involved agree on the planned accomplishments

Successful agreement on goals involves a three-step process of analysis that includes discussion, compromise, and agreement.

1. **Discussion**–Presentation of wants, needs, and capabilities

2. **Compromise**–Give-and-take between parties

3. **Agreement**–Settling on the goals to be achieved within the guidelines agreed upon

The Three-Step Process

Discussion

The discussion step involves getting all the interested parties together to discuss the "who, what, when, why, where, how, and how much" of the desired goal, as well as the expected outcome. In this step, details are openly discussed so that everyone is assured that the intent and purpose of the goal is to fulfill the stated mission. Once all the elements are openly discussed, areas of agreement and disagreement will be exposed so that the parties can proceed to the next step—compromise.

Compromise

Goal setting requires that a compromise be reached before goals can be achieved. There must be give-and-take between the parties and those who will be responsible for achieving the goal. Compromise is an essential part of goal achievement because it establishes the goal boundaries, the elements of the goal to be executed, and the expected results to be accomplished. Compromise is necessary for reaching agreement.

Agreement

Agreement closes out the compromise step and sets the ground rules for goal execution and the efforts to be expended for goal achievement. Everyone involved must agree on the costs (money and other resources) and benefits (hard and soft), as well as the methods of achieving the goal. Without agreement by everyone involved, the goal may not be reached. Therefore, the most essential element in the early stages of goal setting is communication.

Communication

Communication is the result of your efforts to let other people know what is going on. Goals will be difficult to achieve unless everyone clearly understands the mission and the goals.

Communication is crucial for:

➤ Clarifying goals and objectives

➤ Assigning responsibility

➤ Managing activities

➤ Measuring progress

The Ownership Issue

Who owns the goal can have a critical impact on the prospects for goal achievement. That is, within the context of who sets the goal, it is important to consider how the goal will be established.

There are two general approaches to determine who is involved and how the goal-setting process is conducted:

Bottom-up goal setting: Individuals at lower levels commit to what they can do to achieve the goal.

Top-down goal setting: Management sets the goals for lower levels to achieve.

Each method has pluses and minuses.

Bottom-Up Goal Setting

Although it is frequently more time-consuming and difficult to do, bottom-up goal setting is the preferable method because it puts the goal-setting responsibility where the activity will occur, where the product is made, or where the services are provided.

As discussed earlier, organizations that involve all levels of employees in the creation of goals usually achieve more and better results because of individual commitment to success.

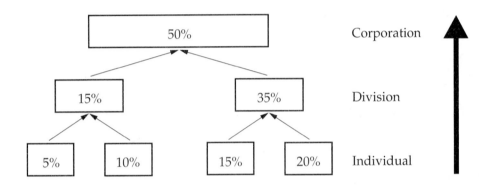

In the example above, each individual commits to the share he or she is capable of contributing. In this case, the four individuals can each contribute 5%, 10%, 15%, and 20% respectively to the next level. This commitment allows the two middle-level divisions to contribute a 15% and 35% share to the goal of a 50% increase.

Top-Down Goal Setting

The goals to be achieved by lower levels in an organization are dictated by the management in top-down goal setting. Management may use top-down goal-setting techniques to reflect the needs of the organization as a whole (the need for sales and profitability, customer service, and so on). These top-down goals are used to determine the specific contribution required at lower levels.

The expected results of the top-down goal-setting method can be the same as those achieved by a bottom-up method. Note that the values in the example below are the same as those shown in the bottom-up example. On the surface, the only difference between the two examples appears to be the direction of the arrow.

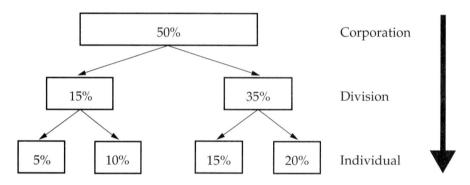

When the top-down goal-setting method is used, the needs of the organization are dictated by management. This often precludes the necessary communication involved in the discussion, compromise, and agreement phases, which create the ownership and team effort necessary for successful goal achievement by those at lower organizational levels.

Remember, active participation in the goal-setting process by ALL the individuals involved is the surest method for success. Only the bottom-up approach recognizes the importance of creating participant ownership as a way of producing the most critical element for goal achievement: personal motivation.

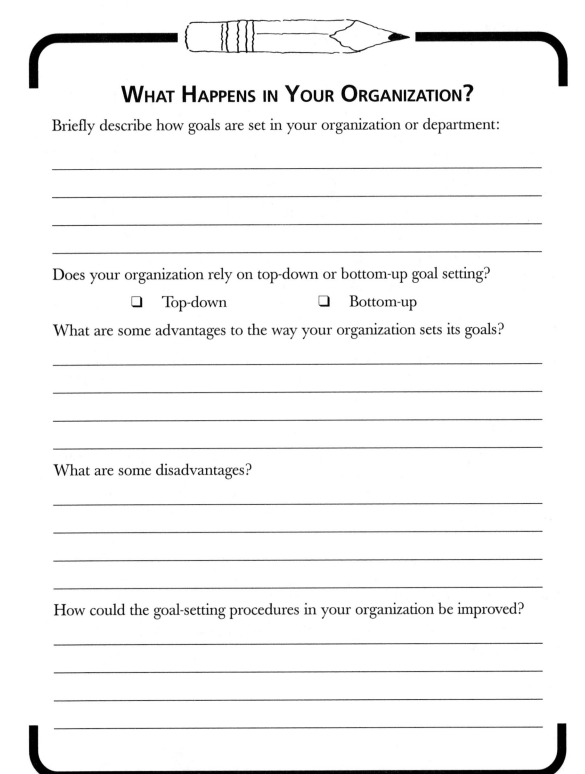

WHAT HAPPENS IN YOUR ORGANIZATION?

Briefly describe how goals are set in your organization or department:

_____

_____

_____

_____

Does your organization rely on top-down or bottom-up goal setting?

❑   Top-down   ❑   Bottom-up

What are some advantages to the way your organization sets its goals?

_____

_____

_____

_____

What are some disadvantages?

_____

_____

_____

_____

How could the goal-setting procedures in your organization be improved?

_____

_____

_____

_____

Adopt and Adapt the Goal

In life and business goal-setting situations, we aren't always the ones setting the goal. We are often assigned the individual tasks we are expected to achieve. For example:

Meeting division sales quotas

Reaching scholastic benchmarks (passing grades)

At other times, we don't have total and complete control over our assigned goals, such as:

Participating on a team to develop a new product

Whether or not it's our own choosing, or whether we work independently or collectively, fulfillment of an assigned goal becomes our responsibility.

So how do you motivate yourself to achieve *someone else's goal?*

First, translate the high-level goal down to your level of responsibility. That is, if you are part of the marketing department, find the marketing aspects of the high-level goal to take on as your responsibility.

Next, adopt and adapt!

You must adopt specific goal-achievement tasks—or the relevant parts of a team task—as your own by thinking, talking, and acting as if they were your own ideas. This helps create the positive vibes necessary for you to follow through with your goal responsibilities. This approach is also helpful in team environments where positive group dynamics can increase both personal and team motivation.

Then, adapt the goal, that is, find a way to actually make it your own. For example, don't focus on the "division sales quota," concentrate instead on your piece of the sales bonus pie when that quota is met. Don't focus on "passing grades," think about the prestige associated with graduating with honors from that special university you enrolled in. Or, imagine the promotion and salary increase that awaits you as a result of the successful new product.

Regardless of how a goal is formulated: top-down, bottom-up, assigned, volunteered, or tasked, you must make the imposed goal manageable (translate it to your management level), find a way to consider the goal your own (adopt), and then identify some beneficial aspect of the goal that is truly yours to accomplish (adapt), if you hope to achieve it.

The key points for achieving imposed goals are:

➤ Translate the goal into an individual goal

➤ Adopt the goal as your own

➤ Adapt the goal to a personal benefit

We'll discuss this more in the motivational sections ahead.

How Are Goals Set?

A Four-Task Process

Goals evolve from a discovery process in which you identify business or personal needs, establish your public or private roles, or review the responsibilities of your job or life to find accomplishments that you want to achieve. When you uncover the *who, what, when, how,* and *how much* of a particular idea, you have the raw material for goal setting.

Goal setting is a sequence of events that enables the creation of attainable, actionable, and rewarding goals that lead to positive results.

Creating goals is a four-task process:

Task 1: Identify opportunities for goals

Task 2: Write goal statements

Task 3: Develop goals

Task 4: Formulate action plans

The pages that follow describe each of these goal-setting tasks.

Task 1: Identify Opportunities for Goals

Questions: *Where are specific goals found? Where does an organization or individual find the best opportunities for creating goals?*

Answer: *All around you and the organization!*

Goals can evolve from almost any aspect of your business or personal life so long as they contribute to the fulfillment of your organizational or individual mission.

There is so much around us that we can use to produce meaningful, worthwhile goals that it is sometimes helpful to focus on a smaller part of the goal opportunity universe. One way to focus is to consider the motivation factor. If motivation is a key factor in goal achievement, then we should seek out goal opportunities in areas that contain built-in motivators.

Some primary areas that contain built-in motivators for goal opportunities are our:

> **Needs**

> **Roles**

> **Responsibilities**

Task 1: Identify Opportunities for Goals: *Needs*

Our needs are perfect starting points for goals because they contain an abundant source of relevant and challenging opportunities.

More importantly, a *need* motivates us to *act*.

Abraham Maslow identified a hierarchy of needs that recognized the strong motivational influence of human activities, from basic survival, to overachievement, to self-fulfillment. Maslow's Hierarchy of Needs has *survival* as its lowest need level. Other levels include safety, love, and worth, leading up to total fulfillment represented by the need for self-actualization.

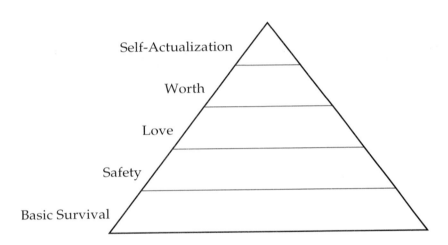

As humans, we can experience need at all five levels. Usually however, our lower-level needs must be satisfied before we are motivated to direct our energy toward a higher-level need (that is, a person will satisfy his or her hunger before seeking out ways to be physically comfortable).

Needs are related to our goals because we work harder to reach a goal that satisfies our unfulfilled needs. That is, we willingly and purposefully direct our energies toward our most pressing needs.

Maslow's Needs in Our World

While Maslow described the Hierarchy of Needs as survival, safety, love, worth, and self-actualization, we often see these needs in our lives in the search for:

➤ **Power**—There is a need to control our own destinies. Power goals can include mastery over tasks or people.

➤ **Knowledge**—The universal desire to know and understand the world around us.

➤ **Recognition** and **status**—People want to stand out from others. This causes us to be attracted to objectives that enhance our ability to be recognized.

➤ **Achievement**—The desire to do something worthwhile for its own sake.

➤ **Security**—We seek to reduce the dangers around us.

➤ **Money**—We want to increase our incomes, i.e., we create goals that lead to greater wealth or guarantee survival.

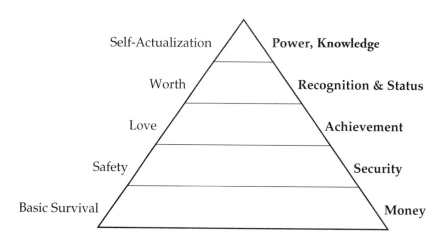

Each of these categories can provide direction for creating worthwhile goals at both the personal and corporate levels. For example, a desire/need to have enough money to take an extra-special vacation may require setting and achieving a sales goal resulting in bonus compensation (money). Or, you may use the same sales goal as motivation to work hard to become Salesperson of the Year, thereby achieving recognition and status.

Using "Needs" to Build Goals

Using needs to stimulate goal ideas requires asking a series of questions:

What do I need?

Money? Power? Knowledge? Achievement? Recognition? Security?

What do I have to do and what goals must be achieved to satisfy this need?

Put this answer in the form of a specific goal statement.

What specific actions or tasks must be completed to achieve this goal?

This will provide the information you will need to determine the objectives and to develop an action plan, discussed later.

And finally:

How does the achievement of this goal fit in with my business or personal mission?

This answer ensures the goal and its objectives are complementary to fulfilling the mission.

Business Needs

An example of a business need might be: *I would like to have enough sales and profit to be able to have my own truck fleet and quit relying on other truckers for my deliveries.*

Again, this one statement has numerous potential goals that can be acted upon. For example:

➤ Increase sales

➤ Increase profits

➤ Improve delivery service

➤ Purchase own truck fleet

➤ Become a vice-president

Each idea can become a distinct goal statement.

➤ Increase sales by 5% per quarter for the next year ending March 31, by developing new clients from outside our current market area without adding any additional salespeople

➤ Purchase one new truck every six months beginning April 1, by using increased sales to finance the truck cost, a cost not to exceed 1% of the net sales increase

Write a business need here.

_____

_____

_____

What are some of the potential goals you can develop from this business need?

1. _____

_____

2. _____

_____

3. _____

_____

4. _____

_____

Goals are meant to establish direction for a business or an individual. They provide a firm foundation for building a set of tactics (objectives) necessary to accomplish the goal.

Task 1: Identify Opportunities for Goals: *Roles*

Each of us has roles to play in life. There are two general role categories: public roles (our jobs at work, for example) and private roles (our personal lives away from work).

Most of us have many different public roles. For example, a middle manager in an organization may have the following roles to play:

➤ Associate (to managers above)

➤ Supervisor (to those below)

➤ Colleague (to peers)

➤ Mentor (to specific individuals in or out of the organization)

➤ Worker (for themselves)

➤ Stockholder (in the company)

We can have as many or more different roles in our private world, including:

➤ Husband/Wife

➤ Son/Daughter

➤ Father/Mother

➤ Leader/Coach

➤ Host/Hostess

➤ Spiritual Adviser

➤ Friend/Relative

Each of us can play multiple roles in both our public and private lives at the same time. That is, we can be a husband/father/son/soccer coach at the same time as we are an associate/supervisor/colleague.

The roles we play allow us to identify opportunities for potential goals.

Task 1: Identify Opportunities for Goals:
Responsibilities

The roles we play allow us to identify opportunities for potential goals because there are specific responsibilities associated with each defined role.

Responsibility means being able to answer for one's conduct and obligations. It implies taking action when action is needed, and doing what is necessary to fulfill one's obligation to others, the organization, or to oneself. Responsibilities provide abundant sources for goals.

One example of a private role/responsibility relationship might be:

Role	Responsibility	Goal Seed	Objectives
Father	To raise educated children	Save enough for college education	Buy savings bonds
			Establish an annuity
			Spend less on leisure activities

While a public example could be:

Role	Responsibility	Goal Seed	Objectives
Supervisor	To provide direction to subordinates	Be available to help individuals solve problems	Keep an open door
			Hold weekly meetings
			Do quarterly reviews

Note that a goal seed is only a starting point from which to identify a potential goal opportunity. Each seed needs to be further defined, developed, and completed within the formal goal-setting process.

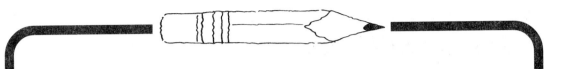

WHAT ROLES DO YOU PLAY?

Name some of the roles you play in both the public and private world.
Indicate a responsibility associated with each identified role.

Private Roles

Responsibility(ies)

_____   _____

_____   _____

_____   _____

_____   _____

Public Roles

Responsibility(ies)

_____   _____

_____   _____

_____   _____

_____   _____

What are some of the potential seeds for goals that you can develop from a
role/responsibility relationship identified above?

1. _____

_____

2. _____

_____

3. _____

_____

4. _____

_____

Task 1: Identify Opportunities for Goals:
Goal Identification vs. Goal Development

In the goal identification phase, it's not important to establish all the details involved with goal achievement or to determine the exact objectives needed to succeed. Those elements are part of goal development (discussed later). The object of goal identification is to determine where an individual or business wants to be in one, two, or five years. The primary objective is to give substance to what would otherwise be only dreams and desires.

Goals are destinations that not only survey where the business or the individual has been and is now, they also combine relevant knowledge with dreams and desires to set a direction for the future. Focus your attention on the ultimate destination. Objectives or milestones are only steps toward the goal. The specific objectives may change as progress toward the goal is made, but the goal itself, once it is established, should remain unchanged.

For example, if the mission is to experience many different cultures and the goal is to travel around the world, then the various destinations (objectives) may change because of travel constraints or the desire to see places not on the original itinerary or in the original budget. But the original goal–to travel around the world–will not change.

On the lines below, write down a personal or career goal that you want to achieve in the next two years.

_____

_____

Now list three objectives you will use to measure the progress you are making toward your goal.

1. _____

2. _____

3. _____

Task 1: Identify Opportunities for Goals:
Goal Types

When you are identifying goals, it is helpful to categorize different goals by type. This clarifies their importance to the mission. There are three types of goals, each of which differ in the contribution they make to the declared mission:

➤ *Essential goals* are necessary for continued, ongoing progress

➤ *Problem-solving goals* propose a more appropriate or desired condition

➤ *Innovative goals* make something good even better

When you understand goal types, you will be able to identify the possible opportunities that are all around, and you will be able to determine the relative importance of the opportunity to the individual or the organization.

Let's investigate goal types in more detail.

Essential Goals

An essential goal identifies everyday activities that require improvement and must be fulfilled to ensure successful results. Essential goals are the recurring, ongoing, repetitious, and necessary activities of business or personal life. These activities are essential to ongoing success.

For example: *Review yesterday's results by 9:00 A.M., and correct errors before new work begins.*

Can you think of an essential goal that you must accomplish on a regular basis? (Hint: Getting up on time tomorrow may be part of an essential goal, if it's to ensure you'll be on time for an important meeting.) Write it here.

_____

_____

Sources of essential goals can usually be found in one's area of responsibility. Assess the tasks you're responsible for to uncover those elements that must be dealt with on a regular basis. For example, if your area of responsibility is sorting the mail, then you must set goals for specific activities such as efficient mail sorting, timing considerations, and effective delivery routes.

Essential goals are those that must be accomplished on a routine basis.

Problem-Solving Goals

A problem-solving goal identifies a current problem or opportunity along with a more appropriate or desired condition. It is a statement of a current situation and a future situation once a solution is implemented. Problem-solving goals outline actions necessary to improve performance. They are vital to growth, but probably not essential to survival.

For example: *Reduce the number of mismatched invoices from 50% to 20% of the invoices received by the end of the 4th quarter, 2003, with no additions to headcount.*

This statement outlines the problem (50% mismatches in invoices received) and the more appropriate or desired condition (only 20% mismatches) that needs to be achieved.

Can you think of a problem-solving goal that ought to be accomplished? Write it here.

_____

_____

_____

Sources for problem-solving goals are:

➤ Aspects of the task that can be improved, such as productivity, efficiency, or accident prevention

➤ Less-than-effective use of time or resources

➤ Obstacles in the workplace that can be eliminated

Ask yourself: What's involved in solving these problems? The answer to this question can provide the seeds for developing problem-solving goals.

Innovative Goals

An innovative goal improves the current condition. Innovative goals are not problems, but rather the result of thinking about making something good even better. They identify activities to be done better, faster, cheaper, easier, or more safely.

For example: *Introduce a change to the existing computer-buying system that will reduce the number of hours needed to determine promotional quantities by the end of the 2nd quarter, 2003, using existing programs to keep development costs below $10,000.*

This statement says that there may be nothing at all wrong with the current condition, but that if improvements could be made, then the system would be better and promotional quantities could be determined more easily than before.

Create an innovative goal and write it here.

_____

_____

_____

Other Potential Areas

Many other aspects of business or personal life can provide opportunities for goal creation. For example:

➤ **Profitability.** Increasing profitability may require essential, problem-solving, or innovative goals to maintain or obtain higher yields from existing sources. Focus on profitability from two perspectives: cost control and higher prices. Both will yield more profit, therefore profitability provides two different elements for potential goals.

➤ **Self-improvement.** Self-improvement may mean finding additional areas of interest, or new responsibilities, to be added over the course of a career. These are personal goals that you may want to accomplish in one year, two years, or five years from now. Setting intermediary essential or innovative goals can help you attain these personal goals.

➤ **Market conditions.** Analyze the needs of your market area to create problem-solving or innovative goals. Analyze customer needs, uncover market weaknesses, and identify market advantages.

Task 1: Summary

➤ Goals can be anything so long as they contribute to the mission of the individual, the business, or the organization.

➤ Goals identify the direction of the organization or individual; they are the ultimate destinations of our dreams, needs, and desires.

➤ Goals are developed from needs, roles, and responsibilities. They can come from our business or our personal lives.

➤ Goals should not change once they are set. However, objectives to reaching goals can and should change as conditions change.

➤ Essential goals must be accomplished for the success of the organization or the individual.

➤ Problem-solving goals ought to be achieved to correct ineffective conditions and thereby produce better results.

➤ Innovative goals are those we would like to accomplish in order to make something good even better (faster, cheaper, safer, or easier).

Essential goals should not be passed over to achieve the relatively less important problem-solving or innovative goal types. Innovative or problem-solving goals should not jeopardize your ability to achieve essential goals.

Try to find opportunities to achieve multiple goals by completing objectives that are common to two or more goals. Obviously, this requires careful planning and written statements that you can mix and match as needed.

Putting Task 1 into Practice

Remember: The purpose of the identification task is solely to un-cover the wants, needs, and desires for future personal or business accomplishments.

Personal desire: *I would like to learn a foreign language so that I can travel to different parts of the world and experience new cultures.*

Possible goal seeds: Learn the French language. Travel to France and experience French culture. See the Eiffel Tower.

Goal type: Innovative. *It would be nice to know how to speak French while traveling in France. My travel would be much easier if I knew the language.*

Goal objective: Self-improvement.

Task 2: Write Goal Statements

A well-defined goal statement is the foundation for goal achievement. The goal is only as good as its statement of needs, desires, and intent to:

➤ Fulfill one's responsibilities

➤ Solve a problem

➤ Be creative and innovative

➤ Satisfy the personal or organizational mission

A goal statement formalizes:

➤ *What* is to be accomplished

➤ *Who* will be involved

➤ *When* the activity will be completed

➤ *How* much it will cost and what resources will be used

Using the S.M.A.R.T. method ensures all these elements of a well-defined goal will be included in each goal statement. The S.M.A.R.T. goal statement is:

Specific

Measurable

Action-oriented

Realistic

Time- and resource-constrained

A goal statement that contains each of these elements will provide an excellent basis for setting and monitoring progress and achieving the goal.

Task 2: Write Goal Statements:
S.M.A.R.T. Goals Are Specific

Specific means detailed, particular, or focused. A goal is specific when everyone knows exactly what is to be achieved and accomplished. Being specific means spelling out the details of the goal. For example:

➤ "Increase productivity" is too general for a goal statement because it does not provide any specific information about what is to be accomplished

➤ "Increase staff productivity" is more specific, because it narrows the scope of the desired outcome

But to be the most specific, a goal statement should say something like: *Increase the data-entry output (productivity) of the staff.*

This last statement specifies the desired improvement and leaves no doubt about what is to be accomplished. Specifying the expected end result is the first step toward creating a S.M.A.R.T. goal.

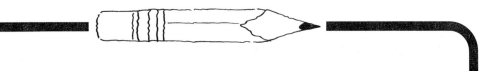

HOW SPECIFIC IS THE GOAL?

Rate the following statements by placing a check (✔) in the appropriate column. Are they specific enough to spell out the details of the desired goal?

	Too General	Not Specific Enough	More Specific
A. Wash and clean the car.	❑	❑	❑
B. Wash and clean the car each week.	❑	❑	❑
C. Wash and clean the car inside and out each week.	❑	❑	❑
D. Get better grades in school.	❑	❑	❑
E. Get better math grades in school.	❑	❑	❑
F. Get at least a B in math in school each semester.	❑	❑	❑
G. Study more often.	❑	❑	❑
H. Study my assignments every day.	❑	❑	❑
I. Study my math assignments at least one hour each day.	❑	❑	❑

Write an example of a *specific* end result.

_____

_____

Compare your answers with the author's suggested responses in the back of the book.

Task 2: Write Goal Statements:
S.M.A.R.T. Goals Are Measurable

Measurable goals are quantifiable. A measurable goal provides a standard for comparison, the means to an end, a specific result; it is limiting. Each goal must be measurable—it must have a method for comparison that indicates when the goal is reached. Doing something "better" or "more accurately" does not provide the quantifiable measurement necessary to determine goal achievement. These words are too ambiguous for a measurable outcome.

For example, "increase the data-entry output of the staff" is a specific statement, but to be measurable, it needs the addition of ". . . to 40 completed orders per day." The words "40 completed orders per day" provide a standard for comparison and progress measurement.

Counting the completed orders each day will indicate the progress made toward the goal and will determine when the 40-orders-per-day goal is reached.

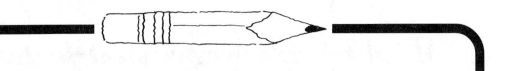

WHICH IS A MEASURABLE OUTCOME?

Check (✔) **Yes** or **No** to indicate whether each of the following is a measurable outcome.

		Yes	No
A.	Provide better service to all my customers.	❏	❏
B.	Answer every letter received within five work days.	❏	❏
C.	Significantly reduce the number of complaints.	❏	❏
D.	Lower the number of complaints by 50% of current levels.	❏	❏
E.	Add only very productive individuals to the staff.	❏	❏

Remember: Measurable outcomes must be quantifiable, a standard for comparison, and limiting.

Write a *measurable* outcome here.

_____

_____

_____

Compare your answers with the author's suggested responses in the back of the book.

Task 2: Write Goal Statements:
S.M.A.R.T. Goals Are Action-Oriented

An *action-oriented* goal is a goal statement that involves an activity, a performance, an operation, or something that produces results. Action verbs describe the type of activity to be performed. Here are some examples of action verbs:

evaluate	**investigate**
appraise	**influence**
inform	**restrict**

For example, in the statement "increase the data-entry output," the verb "increase" indicates that the expected result is to raise the productivity from the existing level to a more desirable level.

Action Verbs

A list of common action verbs is shown below. Place an **X** next to the words found in your business or industry.

act on	evaluate	match
activate	establish	negotiate
add	forecast	purchase
answer	formulate	provide
appraise	gain	produce
authorize	implement	prioritize
change	improve	process
correct	increase	plan
create	invest	quantify
classify	investigate	qualify
complete	incorporate	research
clarify	influence	review
construct	interview	revise
determine	identify	restrict
do, make	introduce	reduce
document	learn	select
develop	lose	secure
define	make	sign up
expand	monitor	support
enroll		

What are some other action verbs common to your business or industry that are not included in the list above?

Write them here.

_____ _____ _____

_____ _____ _____

Task 2: Write Goal Statements:
S.M.A.R.T. Goals Are Realistic

Realistic goals are practical, achievable, and possible. Goals must motivate people to improve and to reach for attainable ends. For a goal to be motivational, the goal-seeker must feel that the goal can be achieved ("I can do it!"). This realization must occur before effort and energy are applied toward reaching the goal.

For example, "increasing the staff output to 40 completed orders per day" is possible and achievable (realistic) only if the current level of output is 23-30 orders per day. If the current level is only four completed orders per day, the "40 completed letters per day" may not be realistic with the existing staff.

The goal is practical only if a need exists to achieve the goal. For example, if there are no more than 10 orders that need to be entered each day, setting a 40-order goal is unnecessary.

Impossible goals demotivate and defeat the goal-setting process. No one strives for goals that cannot be reached. Goals should not be too easy, either. Easy goals do not motivate any more than unattainable goals.

Realistic goals are a balance between what is hard and what is easy to achieve. They require a stretch and may involve risk in order to reach beyond what is easily achieved. It's that little extra in performance that makes people progress and improve. Stretching creates the necessary balance between the effort required to achieve the goal and the probability of success.

Sometimes it's worthwhile to get feedback from someone who knows you well enough to honestly tell you if you're up to a specific challenge and if your prospective goal is realistic.

> Challenging, realistic goals motivate and encourage higher levels of performance.

REALISTIC OR UNREALISTIC?

Realistic goals are practical, achievable, and possible. Are the following goal components realistic?

	Realistic	**Unrealistic**
A. Swim a mile.	❑	❑
B. Swim across the Pacific Ocean.	❑	❑
C. Hold your breath until you faint.	❑	❑
D. Learn to play the piano in one year.	❑	❑

Compare your answers with the author's suggested responses in the back of the book.

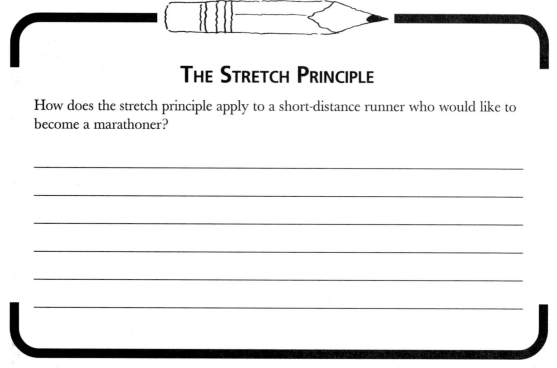

THE STRETCH PRINCIPLE

How does the stretch principle apply to a short-distance runner who would like to become a marathoner?

_____

_____

_____

_____

_____

_____

_____

Compare your answer with the author's suggested
response in the back of the book.

Task 2: Write Goal Statements:
S.M.A.R.T. Goals Are Time- and Resource-Constrained

Time- and resource-constrained means that the time and resources to be expended are scheduled and regulated and that there is a deadline to the action allowed. People generally put off doing things if no deadline is set because human nature always finds something else to do that has a higher priority. Time constraints encourage action to get activities completed. Deadlines encourage activity.

For example, a time- and resource-constrained goal statement might be:

> *Increase the data-entry output of the staff to 40 completed orders per day by June 30, without adding any new data-entry clerks.*

The precise date provides a deadline, while the phrase *without adding any new data-entry clerks* places a limit on the resources used to achieve the goal.

Time constraints and deadlines must be precise to promote the urgency needed to move toward goal achievement.

For example "by the end of October" is more specific than "toward the end of October." But it is not as precise as "by 10:00 A.M. on October 31, (year)." This deadline leaves no doubt about when the goal should be achieved.

Some goals are easily achievable when money and resources are unlimited. We spend until the goal is reached.

For example, one way of achieving the "40 orders per day" goal is to have 40 data-entry clerks available. That assures one clerk for each desired letter. In the real world, however, money and resources are constraints that must be considered in most businesses.

The goal statement must contain resource constraints in order to ensure that there is a practical cost/benefit relationship to goal achievement.

IDENTIFY THE SPECIFIC DEADLINES

Which of the following phrases represent deadlines, and which are just expressions of time?

	Deadline?	
	Yes	**No**
A. Next week	❏	❏
B. Next Thursday by noon	❏	❏
C. As soon as possible	❏	❏
D. First thing Monday morning	❏	❏
E. Before the close of business today	❏	❏
F. Before the close of business today, at 5:00 P.M. PST	❏	❏
G. December 31, (year)	❏	❏

Write your own *precise* deadlines below.

_____

_____

_____

Compare your answers with the author's suggested responses in the back of the book.

Task 2: Summary

S.M.A.R.T. goals ensure that all the necessary elements are included for creating actionable, well-planned, and achievable goals. The S.M.A.R.T. goal is:

Specific: Detailed, particular, focused

> *Increase the data-entry output of the staff...*

Measurable: Quantifiable, providing a standard for comparison and the means to a specific result, limiting

> *...to 40 completed orders per day.*

Action-oriented: Performing, operating, producing results

> *Increase...completed...*

Realistic: Practical, achievable, accurate, possible

> *(Increase)...from current level (20-30 per day) to 40 completed orders per day.*

Time- and resource-constrained: Scheduled, regulated by time, having a finite duration of activity, with limited resources

> *...by June 30, without adding any new data-entry clerks.*

Putting Task 2 into Practice

Remember:

The goal statement is a very important part of goal achievement because it lays the foundation for goal development and execution.

Goal statements must be S.M.A.R.T.

Specific

Measurable

Action-oriented

Realistic

Time- and resource-constrained

Personal desire:

I would like to learn a foreign language so that I can travel to different parts of the world and experience new cultures.

Possible goal statement:

Learn the French language with sufficient fluency to be able to carry on a complete conversation with a fluent friend or a French teacher by December 31, (year), one year and six months from now, within a cost not to exceed $3,000 for books, materials, and courses.

Specific: Learn the French language

Measurable: Sufficient fluency to be able to carry on a complete conversation with a fluent friend

Action-oriented: Learn...carry on a conversation

Realistic: Languages can be learned in an 18-month period with appropriate training and study.

Time- and resource-constrained: December 31, (year), cost constraint of $3,000.

Task 3: Develop Goals

Identifying opportunities (Task 1), and creating S.M.A.R.T. goal statements (Task 2) are two essential elements needed to complete Task 3, goal development.

Goal development expands goal statements to provide context and substance for expected results and benefits. Completion of Task 1 (identify opportunities for goals) and Task 2 (write goal statements) may result in one, two, 10, or 50 legitimate goal statements that will require development before work toward goal achievement can begin.

You should complete goal development for every legitimate goal statement created. There are six steps to effective goal development:

1. **Classify** goals by type

2. **Prioritize** within each type

3. **Establish** standards for performance

4. **Identify** obstacles to goal achievement

5. **Determine** W.I.I.F.M. (What's In It For Me?)

6. **Visualize** achieving your goals

Each of these important and necessary steps to goal development is described in the following pages.

Task 3: Develop Goals: *Classify Goals by Type*

The classification of goals requires a review of each goal statement to determine whether the end result (accomplishment to be achieved) is:

> ➤ **Essential:** Required for the operation of the business or for personal improvement; it must be done.

> ➤ **Problem-solving:** Identifies a less-than-ideal condition and a proposed solution that ought to be done.

> ➤ **Innovative:** An activity that will result in something better, faster, cheaper, easier, or safer.

To classify your goals, create a list of goal statements for each goal type.

Essential goals

Essential goal A

Essential goal B

Essential goal C, etc.

Problem-solving goals

Problem-solving goal A

Problem-solving goal B

Problem-solving goal C, etc.

Innovative goals

Innovative goal A

Innovative goal B

Innovative goal C, etc.

This provides a workable list of identified goals to be achieved.

Goal statements may overlap into multiple types.

For example, a possible overlapping goal statement might be: *Learn the French language with sufficient fluency to be able to carry on a complete conversation with a fluent friend and be able to translate the French instruction materials received with the machinery used in the production plant.*

This innovative goal to learn French takes on an additional problem-solving purpose if knowing French would solve your company's problem of needing a French translator to translate materials each time a new machine is received from the French manufacturer. One motive is purely self-improvement, while accomplishing the goal would also solve a business problem. When this occurs, you need to classify overlapping statements by the highest level of need.

Goal Type	**Level of Need**
Essential	Must be done
Problem-solving	Ought to be done
Innovative	Nice if it could be done

For example, a combination essential and problem-solving goal should be classified as an essential goal because it "must be done," and therefore has the highest level of need. Likewise, an essential/innovative goal is classified as an essential goal. A problem-solving/innovative goal would be included in the problem-solving list because problem-solving goals are more critical than innovative ones.

Task 3: Develop Goals:
Prioritize Goals Within Type

The next step in goal development is to determine the most significant goal to be achieved within each type. Setting priorities results in a list of goals that ensures that the most important goal will be acted on first. Prioritize the essential goals first, followed by the problem-solving goals, and finally the innovative goals, as illustrated below:

	Assigned Priority
Essential goals	Essential goal A
	Essential goal B
	Essential goal C, etc.
Problem-solving goals	Problem-solving goal A
	Problem-solving goal B
	Problem-solving goal C, etc.
Innovative goals	Innovative goal A
	Innovative goal B
	Innovative goal C, etc.

Here are some criteria for setting priorities:

> **Relative importance:** The achievement of essential goal B is objectively more important to the company (or to me) than achieving either essential goals A or C.

> **Time sequence:** Essential goals A and C cannot be achieved until essential goal B is completed, therefore B must have the highest priority.

> **Cost-benefit relationship:** Essential goal B can be achieved at a lower cost than either A or C and will produce immediate benefits. Therefore, B should have the highest priority.

Other objective criteria can be used as well to establish priority within goal types. The key is to establish criteria within each type. There should be no problem-solving goals with a higher priority than the *lowest* essential goal.

If a problem-solving goal (ought to be done) appears to warrant a priority higher than the lowest essential goal (must be done), then one or the other goal statement may be classified incorrectly. Carefully review each goal statement to ensure that a correct classification has been assigned.

Prioritizing is simplified when you have created very specific goal statements. Specific goal statements include *what* is to be accomplished and *why,* along with the expected beneficial results (must be, ought to be, nice to be) and the cost and resource constraints allowed.

This information provides everything necessary to make a judgment on the classification and priority of the goal.

Task 3: Develop Goals:
Establish Standards for Performance

The next necessary step in goal development is to identify a standard for performance that indicates the level of results expected for each goal. Standards of performance serve three purposes:

1. Indicating progress made toward the goal

2. Isolating what remains to be done

3. Telling when the goal has been achieved

It is important that these standards be established before work begins. They represent specific objectives or milestones to be reached during progress. Specific times must be established to indicate when progress will be measured—in future days, weeks, months, or years.

Three separate standards for performance should be established:

➢ **Minimal:** Indicates that some progress has been made toward goal achievement, but it may not be at a pace sufficient to guarantee goal achievement.

➢ **Acceptable:** Progress made is consistent with goal achievement during the time allotted.

➢ **Outstanding:** More progress than expected was achieved when measured at the milestone date. (This level may require elements of risk and reward as motivators to achieving outstanding results.)

For example, if the goal is:

> *Increase staff data-entry output from 24 orders completed per day to 40 orders per day by October 31.*

Then standards for performance might be:

26 orders completed within 3 months = **Minimal**

31 orders completed within 3 months = **Acceptable**

34 orders completed within 3 months = **Outstanding**

OR

32 orders completed within 5 months = **Minimal**

35 orders completed within 5 months = **Acceptable**

38 orders completed within 5 months = **Outstanding**

Remember, standards of performance that serve as objectives will indicate progress by specifying:

➤ When improvement is expected

➤ What the situation will be after it is improved

Proper standards for comparison include a time element for review (within three months) and a quantifiable standard for progress (24 orders per day). Also, remember to establish standards of performance that are realistic and in line with the overall goals and objectives.

Task 3: Develop Goals:
Identify Obstacles to Goal Achievement

Sometimes, there are obstacles to goal achievement. Goals may be blocked by physical, conditional, or psychological obstacles that have to be overcome in order to reach the goal.

Each type of obstacle is a real barrier to goal achievement. It makes no difference if the barrier is tangible (physical or conditional), or solely in one's own mind (psychological)–the barrier is real. Therefore, it is very important to:

    1. Identify the obstacle

    2. Plan a way to overcome the obstacle

Often there are many obstacles to individual goals. It is necessary to identify every possible and conceivable obstacle in order to develop a complete and comprehensive plan for overcoming them and drawing closer to the goal.

Physical Obstacles

Physical obstacles are blocks beyond your immediate control. These obstacles may make it appear impossible to achieve the goal.

For example, physical obstacles that block the goal to "Increase the staff data-entry output to 40 completed orders per day" might be that the data-entry system became inoperative and did not function for an extended period of time.

It is important to anticipate this possibility and have a plan of action ready. What possible steps could be planned to overcome the physical obstacle of an inoperative data-entry system? Write your thoughts here, and check your answers with the author's suggested responses on page 103.

_____

_____

_____

_____

Planning for these possibilities may mean the difference between abandoning the goal and achieving the goal.

Changing Objectives

What changes to the objectives should be considered?

_____

_____

_____

Physical obstacles may be very difficult to overcome because these barriers are real obstacles to the goal itself. Planning for them helps you avoid surprises that can sink goals.

Conditional Obstacles

Conditional obstacles are those where current conditions exist that may make it difficult to attain the goal.

For example: _How can we meet our goal of 40 orders per day while learning a new data-entry system?_

In this scenario, the conditional block is that two tasks need to be performed at the same time. Once again, anticipation and proper planning can help ensure that both tasks can be accomplished. Contingency plans are needed to avoid surprise conditions that can impact goal achievement.

What possible actions could be taken to overcome the above conditional obstacle to goal achievement?

_____

_____

_____

Conditional obstacles may be the easiest type to overcome, because they may only require establishing new objectives or tactics that bypass the obstacle.

Psychological Obstacles

Psychological obstacles are those that exist in your mind. You must believe that the goal can be achieved. If there is doubt about the possibility of achieving the goal, a psychological obstacle is created.

Psychological obstacles are no less intimidating than the more tangible physical or conditional obstacles. They present a real roadblock to the goal seeker. Psychological obstacles are sometimes the most difficult to overcome because they poison your mind.

For example: *Entering 40 completed orders per day is impossible...we'll never reach that goal.*

This kind of thought process is self-defeating and keeps people from starting the goal achievement process. (If you don't start, you can never finish!)

What methods can help overcome psychological obstacles?

1. _____

2. _____

3. _____

For more information on physical, conditional, and psychological obstacles, see the author's comments in the back of the book.

Common Goal Achievement Obstacles

In general, the most common and most dangerous obstacles to goal achievement are *procrastination, unproductive activities,* and *impatience.*

Procrastination

Procrastination is putting off work by waiting for the time to be right—for example, waiting for the right time to change jobs, waiting until the children are older to go back to school, or waiting for the exact moment to approach the boss with a new idea. Conditions may never be perfect. There might always be a reason to wait if you're looking for an excuse to procrastinate.

Avoid the temptation to need perfect conditions. The most perfect time is: **Right Now!**

Another danger of procrastination is inactivity, that is, delaying work and/or taking no actions to bring you closer to goal achievement. Sometimes inactivity is the result of thinking the action required is too big, too difficult, too costly, and/or too risky. To combat inactivity, list the individual steps needed to reach each planned objective. Then, break down these steps into even smaller steps that set out very specific, simple actions that can be completed.

> **Question:** *How do you eat an elephant?*

> **Answer:** *One bite at a time!*

The longer you procrastinate, the more pressure is created on the timeline for goal achievement as expressed in the goal's deadline. Pressure often encourages you to take shortcuts.

Avoid procrastination by:

➤ Having sufficient motivation to achieve the goal.

➤ Establishing clear priorities for identified tasks.

➤ Breaking needed tasks into smaller components.

➤ Setting mini deadlines for each task.

➤ Rewarding yourself when tasks are completed. (This brings the motivation element full circle!)

Performing Unproductive Activities

The second most common obstacle to goal achievement is performing unproductive activities. This obstacle is more dangerous than procrastination because it is harder to detect. This is because, as opposed to inactivity associated with procrastination, there is a lot of activity going on. The problem occurs when activities performed are unproductive, that is, you are working on and completing tasks that are counterproductive to, or bring you no closer to, goal achievement. In this situation, you do things, just not the right things!

Doing the right things means performing those activities that are relevant to the goal-achievement process. These include the specific objectives identified in the goal-achievement planning process. Simply doing something to be doing something gives the appearance of working toward reaching the goal. However, unless the effort contributes directly to, goal achievement, the time and resources invested may be wasted.

Methods which help you avoid performing unproductive activities include:

➤ Establishing clear, focused goal statements

➤ Performing only those tasks that meet objectives and result in moving you closer to goal achievement

➤ Reviewing the results, priorities, and plans that contribute to reaching established goals

➤ Keeping your eyes on the prize to provide you with needed motivation

Impatience

It's a fact of life—some things just take longer to complete that other things!

No matter how long you stare at the oven, to bake thoroughly, the cake needs as long as it takes. You can poke it, prick it, and even take it out of the oven before it's time, but that won't make the cake bake any faster.

Goals are the same way. You can't wait to see some positive results. You don't want to wait for:

➤ The planned steps to be executed

➤ The right resources to become available

➤ The knowledge and experience needed to fully understand the situation

You want results **Now!**

Impatience is a formidable obstacle because it not only short-circuits progress toward goal achievement, but it also causes you to doubt yourself, your capacity to plan, and your willingness to execute.

Combat impatience by refocusing on goal achievement and by reviewing your goal plan to regain your confidence in the objectives and steps you've outlined. Accomplishing the steps should take as long as you've planned (plus or minus some time considerations).

If you have created clear goal statements, outlined specific objectives, broken the objectives into manageable steps, established the necessary goal prerequisites, and delineated the appropriate timelines for each step, then just be patient and follow through on the planned steps to goal achievement.

Practice patience; stay the course you've plotted for goal achievement. There's a reason patience is a virtue...having patience leads to virtuous results!

Task 3: Develop Goals:
Determine W.I.F.M.
(What's In It For Me?)

Many of the obstacles discussed create roadblocks to goal achievement that can result in initial failure, total frustration, and/or premature abandonment of the goal. Obstacles may often cause you to give up before you reach your goals. This happens because interest alone is never enough for goal achievement. Goal achievement requires actions, commitment, and a willingness to persist in the never-ending pursuit of the goal.

In Part 2, we discussed the value of goal ownership, which creates commitment to achieving goals that will fulfill the corporate mission. Commitment however, is a very personal quality. You are more committed to achieving goals you helped create, but you are even more committed to goals that benefit you personally.

Therefore, to achieve success, you must determine:

➤ *What's in it for me?*

➤ *How do I directly benefit from achieving this goal?*

➤ *What are other positive outcomes from achieving this goal?*

While monetary incentives, recognition, pride, and self-empowerment are all good motivators, you are more committed and perform better when you can determine the personal benefits in achieving the goal. Here is an example of both a personal and a business goal:

__Goal__	__W.I.F.M.__
Lose those last 10 pounds.	I'll get to wear all those clothes that don't fit now.
Learn a new PC software program.	I can do my current job faster and it will make me more promotable in the future.

Commitment to goal achievement sometimes means looking at the goal from a more selfish perspective.

Task 3: Develop Goals:
Visualize Achieving Your Goals

Visualization moves W.I.I.F.M. to the next level. The phrase "mind over matter" recognizes the mind as a powerful motivational tool. Visualization helps focus this power to motivate the body and spirit, and further magnifies the power of the W.I.I.F.M. reward. That is, when you visualize (imagine) as vividly as possible, the feelings, sensations, moods, and elation that accompany achieving your goal, you use the power of your active imagination to create positive mental images of the results.

Visualize in brilliant Technicolor and with full sound effects what it feels like to:

> ➤ Listen to the speaker's praise and description of your accomplishments

> ➤ Stand on the podium to accept the award

> ➤ Write out the deposit slip for the bonus check earned

> ➤ Experience a sigh of relief at turning in a completed project report

Scientific studies have proven a direct relationship between visualization and execution. Many Olympic athletes, NASA astronauts, professional golfers, and baseball and basketball players use visualization to enhance or improve their performance.

With the right moods, methods, and milieu, visualization is meditating with a very specific end result in mind. Like meditation, visualization requires practice to produce the vivid images and sensory observations that allow you to "prelive" future experiences.

Set aside the time necessary to visualize the positive end results of your goals. Improve your motivation by seeing the positive rewards that lie directly ahead in goal achievement.

Task 3: Summary

There are six important steps in goal development:

1. Classify goals by type:

> ➤ Essential: Must be done

> ➤ Problem-solving: Ought to be done

> ➤ Innovative: Nice if it could be done

2. Prioritize your goals:

> ➤ Essential goals are more important than . . .

> ➤ Problem-solving goals are more important than . . .

> ➤ Innovative goals

Rank goals within each category based on relative importance, time sequence, and cost/benefit relationship.

3. Establish standards of performance that include:

> ➤ An established time for review of progress

> ➤ A quantitative method for determining progress:

Minimal: Some progress

Acceptable: Enough progress

Outstanding: More than expected progress

4. Identify all obstacles to goal achievement:

> ➤ Formulate contingency plans for overcoming potential physical, conditional, or psychological obstacles

> ➤ Ensure that activities performed are not just busy work but are in fact moving you closer to goal achievement

5. Determine W.I.I.F.M.

There must always be a personal motive identified to ensure motivation and commitment toward goal achievement, especially in business.

6. Visualize achieving your goal to enhance the motivational power of W.I.I.F.M.

Putting Task 3 into Practice

Remember:

Goal development expands the goal statement to provide context and substance for the expected results and benefits. Let's demonstrate the five steps in goal development.

Goal statement:

Learn the French language with sufficient fluency to be able to carry on a complete conversation with a fluent friend or a French teacher by December 31, (year), one year and six months from now, within a cost for books, materials, and courses not to exceed $3,000.

1. Classify: Innovative.

There is no pressure to learn French. I want to learn the language in order to make it easier to travel in France and visit the Eiffel Tower.

2. Prioritize

I cannot quit my job to study French full time, therefore, my first priority is my job. However, in terms of my free time, I would like to give this a very high priority. I am willing to devote two or three nights per week to formal French classes.

3. Standards of Performance

If I take French classes at least two nights per week, after three months, I should be able to listen to and understand at least 50% of a conversation by other students.

After six months, I should understand 90% of what is said and participate somewhat in the conversation.

After one year, I should be able to understand a conversation totally and fully participate in a discussion with other students.

After 18 months, I will converse fluently with the teacher or a native of France with little difficulty.

4. Obstacles

Physical Obstacle: Finding effective training.

How to Overcome: Seek out references and conduct an investigation and interviews for possible schools.

Conditional Obstacle: Business travel may conflict with course schedule.

How to Overcome: Discuss with teacher and get assignments ahead of travel; arrange make-up classes; postpone unnecessary travel.

Psychological Obstacle: Learning a foreign language is difficult. I never studied language in high school or college.

How to Overcome: Sit in on a class to determine how difficult it will be to study; recognize that people do learn languages. Commit yourself to studying and doing what is necessary to learn the language.

5. What's In It For Me?

After achieving this goal, I will be bilingual. I will be able to travel in France with more confidence. I will have a skill that makes me more promotable.

Task 4: Formulate Action Plans

The final task of the goal-setting process incorporates Tasks 1, 2, and 3 into a workable action plan. This plan details the activities and actions necessary to accomplish the goal. Action plans organize thoughts into logical and executable action items (objectives). They describe the objectives to be reached and the tactics to be used to achieve the desired expectations for each goal. When objectives and tactics are incorporated into a workable action plan, goal achievement is more likely to occur.

The first step in the creation of a written action plan is a final review of the goal information available to ensure that it is complete, clear, and realistic enough to serve as the foundation for focused action and activity. When you have gathered the basic material for each goal and goal statement, ask the following questions:

➤ Is the goal complementary to the mission? Does it contribute to the overall purpose?

➤ Is the goal realistic? Is it practical, achievable, and possible?

➤ Did the individuals responsible for achieving the goal participate in its creation?

➤ Have outcomes been quantified so that progress can be measured? This should include when and how much progress is expected.

➤ Are the objectives defined for reaching the goal? How will the goal be achieved?

➤ Are sufficient resources committed for reaching the goal? Resources should include the required people, funding, equipment, commitment, etc.

➤ Do I have the skills, knowledge, and information needed to achieve this goal? If no, how/where can I gather what is needed?

➤ Are potential obstacles to the goal identified? Have contingency plans been designed?

➤ Have I made any invalid assumptions about this goal or the steps to goal achievement?

If you can answer yes to each of these questions, then the action plan will provide a road map to goal achievement. Each of the above elements will be scattered throughout the working papers and goal statements developed in the earlier tasks of the goal-setting process.

The purpose of formulating an action plan is to provide order and organization to the important details of each goal. Order and organization are best achieved using the action-planning form shown on the next page. This form helps to create a road map to goal accomplishment.

82

Task 4: Formulate Action Plans:
Goal Action Form

Once a review is finished and there is reasonable assurance that all (or most) of the necessary goal-oriented details exist, the next step is completing the Goal Action Form. This form is useful because it documents an action plan for goal achievement and acts as a checklist for monitoring progress. The form can also be used during periodic reviews to measure actual progress made (plan vs. actual).

GOAL ACTION FORM

Goal:	Rationale for this goal:

Planned activities: (Steps, Procedures, Assignments)   **Deadlines:**

1.	1.
2.	2.
3.	3.
4.	4.

Projected results (Success Indicators)

❑ Immediate:

❑ Long-Term:

Obstacles/constraints:

Costs (Dollars, Time, Resources)

Person responsible:	Completion date:

Task 4: Formulate Action Plans:
Completing the Goal Action Form

There are eight separate entry areas of the Goal Action Form. Each information element was outlined, defined, or acquired during the earlier tasks of opportunity identification, goal statement creation, and goal development. Here is the information required:

Goal

Enter the actual goal statement created in Task 2. This statement contains S.M.A.R.T. goal elements: specific, measurable, action-oriented, realistic, and time- and resource-constrained.

Rationale for this Goal

Describe the importance of the goal to the overall mission as a guide to the rationale.

If the goal type is:

> **Essential:** The goal is necessary for continued growth and progress of the business or individual.

> **Problem-solving:** Proposes a more appropriate or desired condition than the condition that exists. It eliminates a problem that hinders growth, progress, creativity, improvement, etc.

> **Innovative:** Makes something already satisfactory quantifiably better, faster, cheaper, easier, safer, etc.

The goal rationale should also include the W.I.I.F.M. identified in goal development. The personal benefit to goal achievement (especially in a business environment) is an important motivator that ensures success.

Planned Activities (Steps/Procedures/Assignments)

List the specific objectives that must be met. This is the most important aspect of the action plan because it outlines the specific and measurable steps to reach the goal, as well as the methods to be used. This section should also include the approaches (tactics) necessary to satisfy the needs for goal achievement.

Deadlines

Deadlines are time limits allowed for completion of objectives and the goal. Precise deadlines encourage action and establish the priority of each objective.

Projected Results (Success Indicators)

List the long- and short-term expected results that indicate progress and/or completion of the objectives and the goal. These quantifiable elements provide a standard for comparison and milestones for measuring progress.

Obstacles/Constraints

List the potential physical, conditional, and psychological obstacles that could block progress. The contingency plan and tactics necessary to overcome these obstacles should be detailed on an Obstacles Worksheet. (You will find a blank worksheet on page 85.)

Cost (Dollars, Time, Resources)

State the allowable expense for achieving the goal in dollars and resources to be used. A cost and resource constraint ensures that an acceptable return on investment exists for this goal.

Person Responsible

Identify who is responsible for achieving the goal. Many individuals participate in achieving specific objectives, but only one individual can be held accountable for goal accomplishment.

Completion Date

State the exact date and time for goal completion. This information is part of a properly constructed goal statement.

The completed Goal Action Form organizes the various elements of the goal into an orderly, workable road map for goal achievement. It provides a visual representation (and reminder) of all the actions, activities, expected results, timing, benefits, responsibilities, and contingencies of a well-planned goal.

OBSTACLES WORKSHEET

Some obstacles to goal achievement that are expected, probable, or likely to occur are:

Obstacle: _____

_____

Solution: _____

_____

Actions to implement solutions: _____

_____

Obstacle: _____

_____

Solution: _____

_____

Actions to implement solutions: _____

_____

Obstacle: _____

_____

Solution: _____

_____

Actions to implement solutions: _____

_____

Task 4: Summary

Action plans bring all the elements of goals together to create a useful road map to goal achievement.

Achievement of goals has a better chance for success when the goals are:

> ➤ Clear, realistic, and complementary to the mission

> ➤ Correctly constructed and documented

> ➤ Properly developed

> ➤ Supported by workable objectives

> ➤ Incorporated into a written action plan

Goal Action Forms are helpful devices for organizing the diverse elements of goals into a complete and integrated package.

The form provided on page 85 provides a handy reference and reminder sheet for ensuring goal accomplishment.

Putting Task 4 into Practice

Remember: The action plan is your road map to goal achievement. Plan each step. Clearly define and state the actions and activities necessary for reaching your goal. A plan helps you take action in a way that ensures goal achievement.

Goal Achievement

The Foundation and Support for Goal Achievement

The four tasks—1: Identify Opportunities, 2: Write Goal Statements, 3: Develop Goals, and 4: Formulate Action Plans—are only the foundation for goal achievement. They lay the groundwork by setting the stage for success.

Goals are achieved only through actions and activities. Good planning can tell you how and where to go—but it won't help you succeed unless you put the plan into action.

There are three action elements necessary to ensure goal achievement:

1. **Implement the plan**—the programs, procedures, policies, etc.

2. **Monitor progress**—made at specific intervals, check on actions taken and results achieved

3. **Revise objectives**—as necessary, raise objectives and tactics to overcome obstacles

When executed properly, these three elements create a self-correcting loop for goal achievement.

Implement the Plan

Planning is a good start on the road to goal accomplishment. The new ideas, procedures, policies, and programs, however, must be implemented for progress to be made. It is easier to take action when you have completed the Goal Action Form, because it serves as the road map that specifies *who, what, when, how,* and *how much* for each goal.

➤ *Who* is assigned the responsibility for coordinating the activities needed for reaching objectives

➤ *What* is to be accomplished

➤ *When* the activity must be completed

➤ *How* the goal will be achieved and what obstacles/constraints could block achievement of the goal

➤ *How much* is the cost in dollars, resources, and personnel time to be expended to achieve the goal

All the elements of the Goal Action Form outline the actions necessary for goal accomplishment. However, only real actions and activities will accomplish the goal.

> *The journey of 10,000 miles starts with but a single step.*—Chinese proverb

Goals cannot be achieved solely through planning and wishing. Goal accomplishment requires action and implementation of the positive programs, procedures, and policies that make it possible to achieve the desired goal.

Monitor Progress

Achieving established objectives and goals requires careful periodic monitoring of the actions taken as well as measuring the results of these actions. Monitoring confirms that time and effort are producing the intended results. Also, monitoring actions and progress enables you to see which tactics work best, as well as what changes may be required to get back on track for goal achievement.

The *Activity/Result Monitoring Worksheet* on page 93 is a helpful tool for doing periodic checks on the progress of planned activities. Here is an overview of the information that should be included:

Activity: Information taken from the Planned Activities, Deadlines, and Projected Results sections of the Goal Action Form on page 82.

Relates to Goal and Mission: A list of the complementary relationships that exist between objectives, goals, and mission.

I Expect this Result to Occur: Use for the quantifiable and measurable standards of performance established in the goal statement and goal development phases.

By this Date: Reflects the milestones (dates) set for review of the tangible progress made toward task completion. It is important to set the monitoring milestones at practical and planned intervals. They should be clear and precise calendar dates.

Actual Result: Indicates the status of the activity being monitored. This is a very important element because it will tell whether midcourse adjustments are necessary to the objectives and tactics needed to ensure goal success.

If specific results toward goal achievement are not achieved within the specified time period, it is very important to dissect the causes and events that kept you from making progress. Analyze what went wrong before revising the objectives. This helps ensure a positive learning experience, as well as understanding how to avoid making the same mistakes again.

Ask yourself:

> ➤ Were skills, knowledge, or information lacking?

> ➤ Could I have reached the objective with more/better resources/tools?

> ➤ Was the goal objective unrealistic in some manner?

> ➤ Did I just not work hard enough to achieve the objective?

If the expected results are achieved, then it's time to reward yourself for a job well done! It's very important to continually reward yourself if objectives to overall goal achievement are met within the established guidelines.

If adjustments or modifications are needed, they should be included in the **Revisions to Be Made** section of this form. These modifications then become new activities in the next round of the implementing, monitoring, and revising cycle of goal achievement.

ACTIVITY/RESULT MONITORING WORKSHEET

Date: _____

Goal Statement:

_____

_____

_____

_____

Activity:

_____

_____

Relates to Goal and Mission . . .

_____

_____

I Expect this Result to Occur . . .

_____

_____

By this Date: _____

Actual Result Achieved:

_____

_____

Revisions to Be Made:

_____

_____

Revise Objectives

To achieve your goals, you sometimes have to revise your objectives and tactics, because the actions and activities taken do not always produce results exactly as planned. Sometimes results fall short of planned expectations.

Part of goal development (Task 3) was to identify obstacles to goal achievement and methods for overcoming each potential obstacle. Even with proper planning and established contingency plans, new unidentified obstacles occur that require changes in direction or method to reach the goal. It may be vitally important to the ultimate achievement of the goal to revise your objectives and tactics.

It's very important to note that the goals themselves should not be changed. The goal is important, or it would not be this far along in the process. The monitoring activity outlined above will identify the most effective tactics—those that produce the most beneficial results.

Circumstances change and so should the plans, objectives, and tactics you use to achieve worthwhile goals. Continually review and revise your Goal Action Form (ideally, once every three months for long-term goals). This creates a useful and dynamic work plan for accomplishing your goals.

Goal achievement occurs only when the following two major elements and seven minor elements are present:

Comprehensive Goal Foundation

1. Identify goal opportunities

2. Write S.M.A.R.T. goal statements

3. Complete goal development

4. Write action plan

5. Implement program

Goal Achievement Activities

6. Monitor results

7. Revise plan

The cycle of implementing, monitoring, and revising should be executed over and over during the goal-achievement process. When you revise your objectives and tactics, you then have to implement a new set of policies, procedures, and programs. This implementation is followed by additional monitoring activities at scheduled intervals that result in additional revisions, followed by new implementations, monitoring, and so on until each goal is achieved.

This cycle must occur as often as necessary to draw closer to achieving your goals. The cycle ends only when the goal is reached.

Goal Achievement

Goals are achieved only through action and activity. The three action elements that ensure goal achievement are:

➤ **Implement:** The *who, what, when, how,* and *how much* definitions of action and activities are necessary for goal achievement. This represents the physical execution of the activities.

➤ **Monitor:** Review progress toward goal achievement. Compare your plan with actual progress. Use quantifiable results and specific milestone dates for review.

➤ **Revise:** Revision of the objectives and tactics when change is indicated. Use tactics that work and draw you closer to your goal. Do not revise the goal; change only the means to achieving the goal—the objectives and tactics. Determine what works and what doesn't. Revise the action plan to be more productive.

Summary

What Is a Goal?

A goal is a specific and measurable accomplishment to be achieved within time and cost constraints. Goals are written statements of intent and results to be achieved. These statements contain:

- ➤ Action verbs

- ➤ Measurable outcomes

- ➤ Specific dates for accomplishment

- ➤ Cost and resource constraints

Mission statements define your cause and provide direction for goals.

Objectives are tactics used to achieve goals. They must be complementary to the goal and the mission.

Why Set Goals?

Well-defined goals enable people to choose, design, and implement their life and work objectives to achieve a mission or life purpose.

Goals will:

- ➤ Establish direction

- ➤ Identify results

- ➤ Improve teamwork

- ➤ Heighten performance

Who Sets Goals?

The parties involved in achieving the goal should help define the goal to ensure success. People are committed to achieving goals they helped create.

How Are Goals Set?

Creating goals is a four-task process:

1. Identify opportunities for goals based on our

> ➤ Needs

> ➤ Roles

> ➤ Responsibilities

2. Write S.M.A.R.T. goal statements

> ➤ Specific: Detailed, particular, focused

> ➤ Measurable: Quantifiable, limiting

> ➤ Action-oriented: Produce results

> ➤ Realistic: Practical, achievable

> ➤ Time- and resource-constrained: Scheduled, regulated by time and deadlines

3. Develop goals

> ➤ Classify goals by type

> ➤ Prioritize within each type

> ➤ Establish standards for performance

> ➤ Identify obstacles to goal achievement

> ➤ Determine W.I.I.F.M.

> ➤ Visualize the sights, sounds, and feelings of goal achievement

4. Formulate action plans

> ➤ Use the Goal Action Form (on page 82) as a road map to goal achievement

How Are Goals Achieved?

Goal achievement requires you to:

1. Implement the plan

> ➤ Planning must be careful and comprehensive

> ➤ Execute the plan

2. Monitor progress

> ➤ Measure planned vs. actual results

> ➤ Determine which elements work and which do not work

> ➤ Understand *why* they worked or didn't work

3. Revise objectives

> ➤ Change tactics, not goals

> ➤ Apply what works

4. Restart the cycle

> ➤ Implement the plan

> ➤ Monitor progress

> ➤ Revise objectives

Continue until your goal is achieved. SUCCESS!

Answers to Exercises

Identify the Goal Elements (pages 6–7)

1. **Action verb:** gain

   Measurable outcome: five new customers, gross sales of $20,000

   Specific date: July 1

   Cost constraint: within budget of $1,000

2. **Action verb:** expand

   Measurable outcome: market share of 5%

   Specific date: December 31

   Cost constraint: without increase in ad expense

3. **Action verb:** secure

   Measurable outcome: two new clients, $30,000 income

   Specific date: June 30

   Cost constraint: no more than 30% of time to service

How Specific Is the Goal? (page 49)

Statements A, D, and G are **too general.** They state only broad intents for action.

Statements B, E, and H are a little more specific, but **not specific enough** to be used in goal statements.

Statements C, F, and I are **more specific** and focus intent on a desired outcome.

Which Is a Measurable Outcome? (page 51)

☐ ☑ A. The outcome cannot be quantified as written. *Better* is a relative term and no indication is given as to what *better service* will mean for each specific customer.

☑ ☐ B. *Five work days* is a measurable outcome. It can be determined whether an answer was or was not given in 4 days or 6 days after it was received.

☐ ☑ C. *Significantly* is too ambiguous a term for goals. It is relative to an undefined standard.

☑ ☐ D. *Fifty percent of current levels* is measurable, assuming the number of complaints received is known.

☐ ☑ E. *Only very* is not measurable or quantifiable.

Realistic or Unrealistic? (page 55)

Whether a goal is realistic or not will, of course, depend on the people and circumstances involved. But based on certain assumptions and generalities, here are the author's responses to these goals.

Realistic statements:

A. Swimming a mile has been accomplished by many individuals. With practice, many people could achieve this goal.

D. Learning to play the piano is also an activity that has been demonstrated and is achievable.

Unrealistic statements:

B. Swimming across the Pacific Ocean is unrealistic, even for expert swimmers.

C. Although holding your breath until you faint is possible and achievable, the author's opinion is that it is impractical and therefore unrealistic. If there were a legitimate purpose for holding your breath until you faint, then perhaps this activity could be classified as realistic.

The Stretch Principle (page 56)

The short-distance runner will gradually build endurance by running a little bit farther each day (the stretch). Eventually, endurance will build so that marathon distances are achievable.

Identify the Specific Deadlines (page 58)

Statements B, F, and G are specific enough to represent deadlines.

Statements A and C are too general to be deadlines.

Statements D and E at first appear to be deadlines, but unfortunately the words "first thing" and "before the close" can be interpreted differently by different people.

Deadlines for goals must leave no room for interpretation.

Author's Comments

Physical Obstacles (page 68)

Some possible options for overcoming the physical obstacle of a data-entry system that becomes inoperative are:

➤ Arranging ahead of time with a data-entry service to help absorb the extra work should your system become unusable

➤ Using temporary data-entry clerks should the automated system not function

Changing Objectives (page 69)

The thoughts for changing objectives must be concerned with how to reach the goal. The goal of "40 orders per day by June 30" cannot be changed. Therefore, you must change the "how."

Once again, think of assigning more temporary employees or using overtime hours until the problems are fixed.

Conditional Obstacles (page 69)

Conditional obstacles like this one might be overcome by changing the work hours and/or the workday schedule. You might also temporarily relax the standards of performance until the crisis passes. Remember that efforts may have to be redoubled after conditions return to normal in order to get back on track and to maintain progress toward the goal.

Psychological Obstacles (page 70)

Methods for overcoming psychological obstacles include:

➤ Conducting a meeting that stresses the possibilities for reaching the goal. Get everyone to express his or her viewpoint, especially any doubters. As a group, develop a positive attitude to goal achievement.

➤ Recalling a past goal that initially appeared to be unreachable but was eventually achieved.

➤ Remembering that goals established by those responsible for achieving them have a much better chance for success. Psychological obstacles can sometimes be avoided by a bottom-up goal-setting process.

Additional Reading

Cairo, Jim. *Motivation and Goal Setting*. Hawthorne, NJ: Career Press, 1993.

Coonradt, Charles A., with Lee Nelson. *The Game of Work*. Salt Lake City, UT: Shadow Mountain, 1993.

Covey, Steven, Ph.D. *First Things First*. NY: Simon & Schuster, 1994.

Covey, Steven, Ph.D. *The Seven Habits of Highly Effective People*. NY: Simon & Schuster, 1988.

Freeman, Arthur, Ph.D. and Rose DeWolf. *The 10 Dumbest Mistakes Smart People Make*. NY: HarperCollins Publishers, Inc., 1992.

Haynes, Marion E. *Project Management, Third Edition*. Crisp Series, 2002.

Jones, Elizabeth F. *You Can Get There From Here*. Nags Head, NC: Washington Publications, Inc., 1990.

Karlson, David, Ph.D. *Marketing Your Consulting or Professional Services*. Crisp Series, 1988.

Klauser, Henriette Anne, Ph.D. *Write It Down, Make It Happen*. NY: Scribner, 2000.

Riley, Lorna. *Achieving Results*. Crisp Series, 2001.

Scott, Cynthia D., M.P.H., Ph.D. and Dennis T. Jaffe, Ph.D. and Glenn R. Tobe, M.A. *Organizational Vision, Values, and Mission*. Crisp Series, 1993.

Waitley, Dennis. *The New Dynamics of Goal Setting*. NY: William Morrow and Company, Inc., 1996.

Wilson, Susan B. *Goal Setting*. NY: AMACOM, 1994.

Also Available

Books•Videos•Computer-Based Training Products

If you enjoyed this book, we have great news for you. There are over 200 books available in the *Crisp Fifty-Minute™ Series*. For more information visit us online at www.axzopress.com

Subject Areas Include:

Management

Human Resources

Communication Skills

Personal Development

Sales/Marketing

Finance

Coaching and Mentoring

Customer Service/Quality

Small Business and Entrepreneurship

Training

Life Planning

Writing